Muffin the Fish

Mu**ff**in the **f**ish was very wide,

With **f**our **f**unny stripes down his side.

He wished he had **f**ingers instead o**f** **f**ins,

Not funny flaps that look like pins.

With **f**ingers, Mu**ff**in could hold a **f**ork,

And i**f** he had toes he could also walk!

Mu**ff**in likes to la**ugh** and visit many places,

To meet other **f**ish and make **f**unny **f**aces.

The other **f**ish **f**ind him very strange,

But Mu**ff**in thinks he's **f**unny, and he won't change.

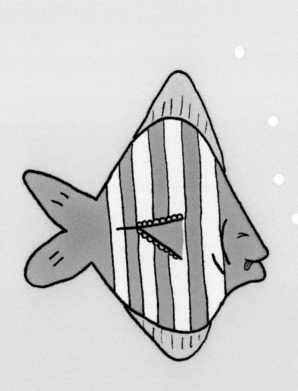

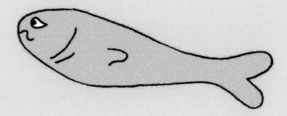

-f-f-f-f-f-f-f-f-f-f-f-f-f- Mu**ff**in flits about,

Finding lots o**f** yummy **f**ood no doubt.

And when a little child **f**eeds Mu**ff**in **f**ood,

He might nibble their **f**ingers i**f**
he's in that kind o**f** mood.

The nibble doesn't hurt – in **f**act it **f**eels like bliss,

Just a flitter and a flutter like a butterfly's kiss.

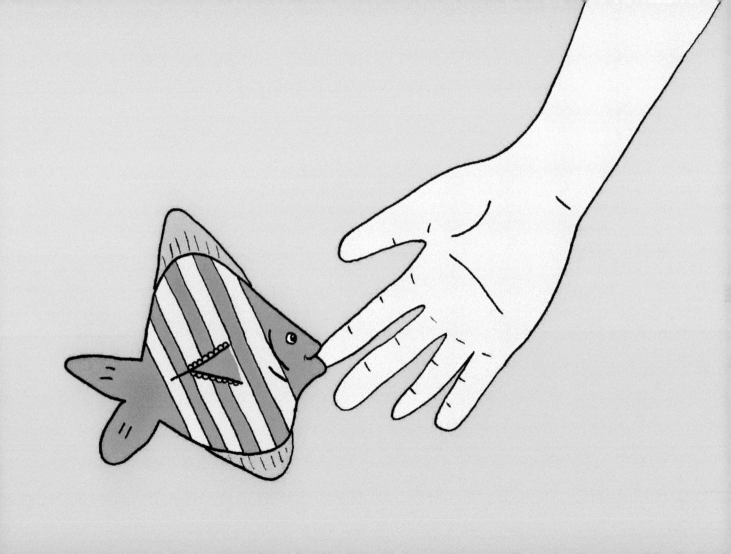